ANCHOR
BOOKS

DANCE WITH REALITY

Edited by

Kelly Oliver

First published in Great Britain in 2002 by
ANCHOR BOOKS
Remus House,
Coltsfoot Drive,
Peterborough, PE2 9JX
Telephone (01733) 898102

HB ISBN 1 85930 964 X
SB ISBN 1 85930 969 0

FOREWORD

Anchor Books is a small press, established in 1992, with the aim of promoting readable poetry to as wide an audience as possible.

We hope to establish an outlet for writers of poetry who may have struggled to see their work in print.

The poems presented here have been selected from many entries. Editing proved to be a difficult task and as the Editor, the final selection was mine.

I trust this selection will delight and please the authors and all those who enjoy reading poetry.

Kelly Oliver
Editor

CONTENTS

DICK TURPIN

Dick Turpin rode his big black horse
Along the King's highway
And when he challenged anyone
There's none would say him nay
His name sparked fear in many hearts
Travellers were wary.
To venture forth in many parts
Was really very scary
His tricorn hat and flowing cloak
Was black as any raven
So travellers in carriages
Were glad of any haven
Now looking backwards down the years
Dick Turpin, he had charm
He never robbed a poor man
And not many any harm.

Dora Watkins

THE DEVIL'S CHILDREN

They don't know any better
They were nurtured by the gun
Their lives are not like 'living'
Clouds envelop all their sun
No music fills their moments
No laughter cuts their stare
Existing for destruction
For they never have a care
No thought for any other
No emotion, no concern
Were their mothers proud to bear them?
What foundations did they learn?
Did they ever 'play' as children?
Smile at rainbows, stroke a pet?
Was their only toy a hand gun
As they never have regret?
Is life truly cheap and worthless?
They mark death on every door
Can't they really see the suffering
Or just wonder what it's for?
Did they never kiss a baby?
Watch a sunset, love a wife?
Don't they ever seek the meaning
Or the reasons they've a life?
Don't they ever dance or giggle
Feel the warmth of precious love?
Are they so hell-bent on terror
They forget in God above?
For he's there and ever watchful
And they will have a price to pay
It is so true you reap the seeds you sow
And so on Judgement Day

They will have to face their Maker
And recount their 'bloody' dawn
There's no martyrdom for killers
Why in God's name were they born?

David Whitney

PRISONERS OF ALCATRAZ

Alone stands the prison on a cold hostile island
Barred windows gaze out like unseeing eyes
A ghostly mist floats across dangerous water
concealing the mysteries the prison wall hides

Alcatraz, home of notorious villains
Thieves, murderers, bootleggers detained long ago
Ultimate punishment is served at the prison
Escape inconceivable as prisoners well know

Robert Stroud, well-known as the Birdman of Alcatraz
Al Capone, gang leader once fearsome and strong
Two infamous gangsters who terrorised their victims
The mighty have fallen and justice is done

A cell for each inmate, dark and degrading
Caged like an animal dangerous and feared
Here they are tamed to conform to the system
Life and endurance is tough and severe

Solitary confinement for those who are mutinous
Big egos deflate as the years pass them by
Monotonous routine is the daily existence
Some will see freedom, others will die

Years have moved on since those days on the island
The prison lies empty, the occupants gone
These hardened gangsters are now part of history
The Alcatraz story forever lives on.

Sheila Wyatt

MY FATHER, MY HERO

My Father was my hero
From the days when I was young
I put him on a pedestal
He made our days such fun
He read a lot
Could relate things
You'd never heard before
Could play an instrument with ease
And songs could write a score
He made us laugh
Did magic tricks
I thought him very clever
Affectionate and warm
He was just the best Dad ever
He was my hero sure enough
Though died when he was young
The love we had for him
Still near
When all he did was done.

Jeanette Gaffney

TO BREAK FREE

A situation? (Come with me)
To break free from a situation,
I will not say, of who, for one
simple reason, it could be you.
We all breathe the same air and
it is free, we are all born into
this world and hope it will shine.
For most of us it will be fine,
for a chosen few we try to break
free from a situation
(Come with me).

Shauna Hamilton

IDOLS

I might draw parallels
between myself
and Scarlett O'Hara,
Elizabeth Bennett,
Anna Karenina,
or Madonna. Ruth loves
Mother Teresa,
and Marilyn Monroe.
Marcus never will
give up on his great idol
Elvis. For nine year old
Kathryn it is
the Spice Girls, Geri,
and Britney. My
verdict? It is
healthy enough to
be obsessed,
in moderation.
Beyond that point . . .?
I really would not know.
Hospitals have wards full
of 'Elvis Presleys' and
'Madonnas',
so we hear.

P Puddephatt

IF I RULED THE WORLD

If I ruled the world
I would cast some spells
If I ruled the world
I would attract love that repels.

If I ruled the world
I would make schools more exciting
If I ruled the world
I would stop the fighting.

If I ruled the world
I would zap new clothes,
So I would have loads.

If I ruled the world
I would make things right
If I ruled the world
For you I would make every day bright.

Samantha Dolley (11)

IF I RULED THE WORLD . . .

If I ruled the world, war would never come,
And that would teach some!

If I ruled the world, sweets would be free,
And adults couldn't drink tea!

If I ruled the world, there'd be no uniform for school,
And people could dress up cool!

If I ruled the world, cars wouldn't exist,
But spaceships, top of the list!

If I ruled the world, asteroids would never hit,
They'd be blown to bits!

If I ruled the world, animals wouldn't die out
And dinosaurs still about!

If I ruled the world I might . . .
Just not have got everything quite so right.

Rachel Leighton (10)

IF I RULED THE WORLD...

If I ruled the world, I would,
Stop all world wars,
Have more serious rules in the police forces,
Demand that the world had nicer school uniforms that
                                    kids would enjoy wearing,
Make the Internet a less expensive place,
Make the environment a cleaner, more healthy way to live,
I would invent charities for the people that have no money,
                                    homes or food,
Insist that peace was made by the USA and Afghanistan,
On the whole, I would try to make the world a better place.

Laura Grant (11)

A WICKED PLAN

A wicked plan
Devised by a man,
September 11th started a war
Now's the time for settling the score.

Aircraft carriers, bomber planes
Neutral observers see their aims.
A world at war, a third one now
It doesn't stop the political row.

Who will win this war of attrition
As the bombers fly their sortie missions?
All of them say 'God is on my side,'
It remains to be seen who He will guide.

If He guides none, what will they do?
On that philosophy I recommend you chew.
For history has been written before time began
Inclusive of all and not just Afghan.

Denise Shaw

ROLE MODEL FOR A MALIGN OLD AGE

Tap!
Tap! Tap!

I hear him coming,
Tap-tapping
Down the street -
Blind Pugh.
I sweat!
His bony grip
I fear.

Yet when my light grows dark
And pleasure thin
It's him I'll emulate -
Blind Pugh,
Tap-tapping street to street
Affrighting my old mates;
And put the 'Black Spot'
On you and you
And you!
And all other wicked, wicked children.

Tap!
    Tap! Tap!
        Tap! Tap!

Terry Smith

PET FAVOUR

The cat broke out of the box and into the hedge it fled,
My superhero didn't leave, chased after it instead.
The cat must have known it was being taken to the vet's,
We were doing a favour for our daughter, we've no pets.

Hero snatched the cat back, it rapidly swung round its head,
Managed to sink its claws in him, my, how his fingers bled.
We placed the cat at the vet's and to the hospital went,
Bravely had an injection, a few words he did vent.

You may only be small of size but I am proud of you,
In my eyes, because of your heroism, your stature grew.
Your enemy might only have been female tortoiseshell,
But my hero, it's a good job from wounds you heal well!

S Mullinger

ROBBIN' GOOD

With all the fighting going on
My kids drew up a list,
Just in case we were the only
Ones left to exist.

My boys would search for other folk
Left hopeless and alone,
Then ask them to collect their thoughts
And join us in our home.

The girls would then prepare a meal
Of which we would divide
Between the people, just like us
Who somehow had survived.

Me? - I'd raid our corner shop.
Take fags, ice cream . . . and beers,
No conscience would my actions have,
- They've been robbin' me for years!

Linda Zulaica

THE SAGA OF DICK TURPIN

With a coat that shone like ebony Black Bess was his horse's name
Her fearless rider the highwayman who is in the annals of fame
Dick Turpin was this man of renown the rich his prey we know
He robbed them on the country roads with a 'Stand and deliver
your gold'
It is said that he loved the maidens and always left them with a kiss
They gave their jewellery willingly and with a shyness puckered
their lips
A reward was posted for his capture and it read *Dead or Alive*
A treacherous friend sold his soul then forever he was despised
Dick languished in Newgate Prison while the gallows and noose
were hung
Many a maid cried and was sad and musicians told of him in song
But still today he's remembered with fondness and even revered
His courage was bold and in tales we are told of Black Bess and the
brave cavalier.

Gillian Mullett

DEDICATED TO DIANA, PRINCESS OF THE PEOPLE
(Died 31st August 1997)

Her gallant soul has but taken flight
She is now enveloped in the Light
Of Jesus Christ, her Lord and Master
She is happy in the Hereafter.

While on Earth, she led a true, good, life
She was a daughter, mother and wife
She did good and had a loving heart
She cared deeply for others, no part
Was truly false, 'cept maybe on show
She hid behind a brave face, although
Her inner agony, hard to bear
Almost too much, she had her share
Of crying to sleep, dreading the day
How she felt inside, who can say?

Yes, she had her yoke, burdens to bear,
But for her children, oh, always there
They were her pride, happiness and joy
Her reason for living, her boys

She bustled about from place to place
Sharing comfort, joy, to each his space
The greatest gift that she could give
Was her time so that others could live
A life of dignity and release
From Life's hardship, she brought Peace . . .
Only for a moment, her smile shone
Like a beacon of hope - world forlorn
Without her, the world's a far worse place
Lady Diana, Lady of grace
Your star will shine for evermore
You are a Legend, of folklore.

Mary A Shovlin

HEARTFELT HEROES

The parents of a special boy,
Who died so tragically,
Amidst their grief and shattered lives,
They let his heart go free.

Their world had crumbled at their feet,
Pain tore them both apart,
But they remember how he'd said,
'I'd like to give my heart.'

They were so brave, remembering when
They'd talked of what they'd do,
If, God forbid, that day should come,
But now it had come true.

No second thoughts, no doubts at all,
His wishes would be met,
Although he's gone, his heart still lives,
We never will forget.

His heart still beats, a life still lives,
A family laughs with joy,
And thank those heroes, oh so brave,
The parents of that boy.

Jim Sargant

TERRORISTS

How can we honestly talk
    to people with no faces,
who disappear or blow themselves up,
    while at the time, holding all the Aces?

How can we recognise
    people who do not exist,
people who want to change the world
    yet will go to their deaths . . . to resist?

How can we value their trustworthiness
    knowing their evil way is to deceive.
Living to maim and to kill is their trade
    and who believe, once they are dead, God receives?

Do we pity mad dogs in their madness,
    who for fun, kill the herds they protect,
or shoot them down as deserving,
    bringing peace, to the flock, the object?

If the world is to be democratic
    and majority votes win the day,
Then these madmen who cause world disruption
    should be silenced now we've heard what they say.

Terrorists doing crimes for religion
    should be told what religion's about.
No God worth a prayer would accept them,
    nor their sins be forgiven, undevout.

So to terrorists I wish all damnation;
    for their crimes may they finish in Hell,
Having worked for the Devil while they were alive
    down in Hell is their right place to dwell.

Leslie Holgate

A Certain Someone Made No One

I knew not your presence,
Yet you must have looked down upon us
Upon that fateful night
With your black, obliterated face
And seen seeds of uncertainty
Sown in soil so cursed,
Seeds which grow into I know not what.
And again your non-eyes open
And it is you I gaze upon,
But I cannot see you
And I can never know you,
Your sowing is now done.

Helen Marshall

SENNA

You had it all, now you have nothing.
I sit in the sun and hear the birdsong that you
Will never hear again.
And your wealth is worthless.
Your villas stand empty, blue pools glistening silently
In the afternoon heat.
Wandering round my terrace cottage, full of bouncing
Springer spaniel, I feel the loss of you.
Hero of the magazines, beloved of the press.
A stranger, worlds apart, though in my living room.
A happy May Day holiday for one who works to live -
Scarred by the death of one who lived to work.
Divided in age by one month, one week, your fate was decided
On May 1st, 1994.
I do not drive, can't stand the lunacy
And cannot comprehend the lightening judgements
That you had to make behind that wheel.
190 miles per hour is inconceivable to me.
If I should sneeze, it would make no difference -
It may have made a lot, piloting a grounded missile, such as yours.
And, through the juddering camera lens mounted at your shoulder,
I safely watched, from my settee -
As you sparked, and slew, and hit, and sheared your monstrous car.
I sat and watched, as bit by bit you were left, in your
Million-pound cockpit, seeing with horror that you did not escape it.
My brow was furrowed with worry, and yours was battered and bloody.
Fate had reached out and pinched the wings of your butterfly-fragile car
And killed you.
I sit in the sun with a heavy heart, but one that is still beating,
And grieve for a hero I never knew.

Denise Holt

TROUBLE ON LEGS

Like a tumble of meerkats with half-open jaws
They sidle onto the train;
A handful of youngsters with gum in their mouths,
The average passenger's bane.

Opportunists, they glance to each side as they range
All ready for nuisance or game,
Each gripping a skateboard and wearing a cap
With a logo to lend them some fame.

A tangle of teenagers grown out of cute
Expensively, carelessly dressed,
They clutter the aisle and monopolise seats
Furtively watched by the rest.

Spotty, lean and untested, with youth on their skin,
Defiantly loud, full of zest.
And the fare-paying passengers covertly glare
At their multiple, unwelcome guest.

Alert to authority, jostling and rude
Adroit at evading all blame;
Remarks fly like missiles from one to the next
In language nocturnal and strange.

Train doors hiss open! Agile in flight,
Swiftly feral, they exit the train.
Into the cautious suburbs they dart,
Escape into darkness again.

Viv Eliz

HEROES AND VILLAINS

I have an angel next to me,
She's always there, for me to see.
When I am scared or alone at night,
She flies around, just in sight.
My angel never flies away
She is my hero to this day.

Janet M Baird

SUPER-DUPER HERO

John Wayne just gunned down three outlaws,
Superman flies at the speed of light,
Batman's just clobbered the joker,
These are all heroes all right.

Bruce Lee kicks butt all weekend,
Van Damme joins in the fun,
The Hulk crashes through buildings,
Clint Eastwood is like lightning with his gun.

Zorro has saved another village,
Robo-Cop clears crooks from town,
All these heroes to choose from,
But who should wear the crown?

Well, I'm sorry, but none of them come near,
I met my hero as a lad,
I have no problem making up my mind,
The man with the crown, was my dad.

Roy Beaman

Lollipop Ladies For Adults

If lollipop ladies and men were endowed with
Much tougher legal powers, they could help shoppers
Cross Oxford -, and Regent Streets; think about that, then!
I wonder why you haven't thought of it yet, Ken
Livingstone? Kerb drill's not just for teenyboppers.

Adults need help crossing strange roads, besides children.
The elderly should have patrols' special care, too,
Between post offices, and bus stops, or cab ranks.
The traffic advances like a parade of tanks,
Heedlessly. The lollipop brigade could imbue
Its members with fair play. Street life performs in turn -
One for the fast movers, one for walkers they spurn.

Gillian Fisher

MEN'S WARD

Today, they say,
There are no knights, no heroes.

But I have seen
Men who quest
To get the best from pain,
Who armour themselves
In courage and persistence
Through the long night's battlefield;

I have seen
Men surmounting illness and despair
Under the banners of cheer and comedy;
And those who, living through
The last long adventure
Prove out the mettle
Of the human spirit.

This ward has housed more knights
Than ever took
The road to Camelot!

Pamela Constantine

'NOW EVERYONE WILL KNOW WHO I AM' - LEE HARVEY OSWALD

Dealey law hovers
But nobody bothers
To check the place where you should be.
Does the barrel still smoke
As you're drinking a Coke
Or dashing downstairs to infamy?
Run red run, there they come!
Ruthless killer? Worthless bum?
They don't know now nor did they then
What you were doing, or why, or when,
But it wasn't all over as you said
Nor when your belly was full of lead.
For you it had only just begun
But had you lost or had you won?
Was somebody hired
For the shots that were fired
And an unloved lamb sacrificed for the bait?
Or did you send away
To keep the pigs at bay
A mail-order death wish that sealed your fate?
Did you get what you deserved,
Your place in history reserved,
Or pretend to be what you were not
For the ones who fired your fatal shot?
In the crowd there shines a jewel
Known to all, but madman or tool?
With Texan justice and all lies true
There will be no fair play for you.

Joanne Starkie

NAPOLEON'S SECRET

Napoleon, Napoleon
His fate was sealed by Wellington.
A prisoner on a distant isle
He was dejected for a while,
But then he had a change of style.
Away from all the cares of state
And petty military hate.
Away from all the strains of war
He found his happiness once more.

After the long Moscow retreat
And Waterloo, the sad defeat
The quiet life was one long treat,
And after all the stress and strife
Now was the best time of his life.

He met a native on the shore
A lovely girl of twenty-four
A life of pleasure now he saw
He now had happiness galore.

Historians were not aware
Of this romantic love affair.
Where all his other plans had failed,
This time alone success prevailed,
And history was not to know
A baby girl would steal the show.
This secret of Napoleon
Was hidden then from everyone.
The mistress of Napoleon
She was the perfect paragon.

John Freeth

MARXISM

Communism's dead!
All of the faces turned red
In the assembly rooms.

'Our hero will have
To lose his head,
Just to be proper,' they said.

Nicola Barnes

BEAST OF A BOSS

This person was a rotten boss
A person who didn't give a toss
What was said to people's faces
Accusing them of false disgraces
There was equal rudeness down the phone
A stream of swear words would drone
However much work you happened to do
You'd be degraded till your esteem was through
That's one reason why the secretary went
Somewhere else hoping to pick up a better scent
The aroma of tension drove her spare
So she could not work there
The manager has no desire to come near me
Because I know the truth as you can see.

Pauline Edwards

THE SHADOWMAN

He comes through the gate.
October's morning gold
is hazy now, his best
sky lies late in bed
thinking of nothing

Sun wades up to his waist
in his languid hours
opulent and replete
plucks his fruit with
hands now wrinkling in

his final days. His eyes
with darkening cataracts,
he strokes his golden skin
now to grey and straggling
hair coils round his sagging

flesh. Unassuaged in his lusty
ways the sun gives in her plentitude
he sighs in ecstasy, wind caresses
his limbs now beginning to gnarl,
turn ancient, calls can hardly

be heard. Deafened, blinded, his
glorious harvest begins to die.
He stands a moment contemplating
dying treasures heaped behind him.

Slowly he closes the gate.
Cold wind whips last final leaves
away.

T Webster

THE ELEVENTH OF SEPTEMBER

It was evil, so naked that it beggared belief,
skyscrapers and bodies falling like autumn leaves;
lives suddenly ended in the business of living,
thousands of souls from their bodies riven.

It was hatred so black that it defied all sense,
terrorism's seal making the present, past tense;
earth's nations reeling at hell's enthral,
death, dust and smoke spreading their pall.

But from the skies 'twixt heaven and hell
came voices of light, their love for to tell;
loved ones, facing earthly extinction
making their last sacrifice a benediction.

And in the chaos of that smouldering hate
men toiled day and night to find their mates;
these lives had been given, freely in love,
showed light conquering darkness, its power to prove.

Catherine Riley

VISIONARY

With long strides he departed
Into the night
Driven by a vision
To put things right
To sweep clean the alleys
Where down and outs strayed
To help all the youngsters
Who with drugs played
He was not a sinner
Nor was he a saint
Just a man with vision
With a world to paint
To right every wrong
To heal every ill
Was his way of giving
His strength and his will.

Margaret Gurney

AD ASTRA

(The Battle Of Britain)

In a wild flight into the lonely sky
You left the world forever. Who can know
What supreme joy you felt where cloud-winds blow,
Before you died alone, so far, so high.
You sought the stars through spaces none can fly,
The rushing winds about the sun. Through death
Who could not steal that last, intensest breath,
You reached the height where those bright stars glide by.
Below, the dark sea swells; below, the land
Lies in black shadow, and the wind and rain
Beat out an endless echo of lost pain;
Beat through the darkness of perpetual night.
But you, who won that far-off, starlit strand
Live now secure amid immortal light.

Diana Momber

PADWORTH GULLY, 1643

(21st September 1643 - The morning after the first battle of Newbury)

Along the ridge from Padworth school
Walk towards the church,
Even summer's heated noon
Is cooled by keen research.

A legacy from civil war
A deep scar on the land
Time has staunched this open wound
Of gallant foolish man.

A troop of horse in Rupert's charge
A thousand musketeers,
Ambushed Essex's trained city bands,
Of death they had no fear.

Essex wearied from the fight
From nearby Newbury came,
A long thin line in early light
Down leafy narrow lane.

No movement greeted listening ear
No scout sent on ahead,
Down this gully men still poured
In hour, three hundred dead!

And now the trump. Of Rupert's force
Rings out across the vale,
Men fell-to with shout and curse
Wielding shot and flail.

But Essex's men stood their ground
Tired though they still might be,
Many volleys finding mark
In Rupert's cavalry!

At length the prince falls back
He must, such slaughter cannot be
One last volley into lane
And back to Newbury!

Meanwhile Essex gathers men,
Struggles on to Theale,
The Kennet crossed at Padworth Ford
To Reading silent steal.

In Padworth churchyard many found
A final rest place here,
The wind that blows through churchyard copse
Still sheds a silent tear.

So if you're walking in the sun
And feel a stiff cold breeze
And down the narrow lane you've come,
Say a prayer please.

Graham K A Walker

THE JOKER

I have been separating for some time,
The wheat from the chaff I feel bereft
Amazingly the chaff on the right became high I found
As opposed to the wheat very little on the left.

No more shall I give anyone the opportunity,
No more a present. No more a future,
I choose to remain with my life totally empty,
I make a very loyal friend, though a terrible adversary.

In future a tattoo upon my forehead
Shall read *prat,* in neon flashing lights
Why, oh why do people believe I will not be misled
So perhaps now is the time to exit to my final bed.

Jay Baker

EARTH WAS A BEAUTIFUL PLANET

Earth was a beautiful planet, until that eleventh day of September,
when cowardly fanatic executioners, turned thousands of lives
into an ember.
Good innocent people of this world, in prominent buildings of
the United States,
had their lives extinguished, orchestrated by Osama Bin Laden
and his mates.

The scriptures built us a picture of Christ's historic birth,
and how God created for us all, the Heavens and the Earth.
They tell us of all the creatures, they were both great and small,
and that the Lord in Heaven above, was the maker of them all.

Thanks to God's creations, we see the birds and bees,
performing for us daily, in the flowers and the trees.
Seasons come and seasons go, Nature's story does unfold,
a show of glowing colours, just like those scriptures told.

We learned that man sailed the seven seas, with great anticipation,
to explore, and later wage war; on many a neighbouring nation.
It was many years ago, man started speaking 'Peace on Earth',
but history has proven so many times; they're words of little worth.

All the beautiful things on Earth, are God's gifts to his creatures,
He created this wonderful world; we should not change its features.
Sadly man made the toxic waste, which flows into our rivers and seas,
and destroying the ozone layer; the good Lord this will not please.

The world was once a beautiful place, given to us by the Lord,
then came this massive destruction; to disrupt our love and accord.
God intended this planet Earth, to be a good place for all to dwell,
these brutal terrorists must be stopped; for Earth has become
a living hell.

Wenn-The-Penn

STREET MAN

Street man is here again,
He appears out of nowhere,
Every morning,
Every night,
He banishes woe from your sight.
A smile in the rain,
A grin in the snow,
A laugh in the wind,
A conversation in the cold.
Street man juggles for the children,
Plays guitar for Dad,
Bows for Gran, and does a little dance.
Street man is a hero for those who are down,
A knight for those who fear they've lost it all.
Street man is the hero who can give everything,
For street man has nothing.

P Benton

TROT, CANTER, GALLOP, CHARGE

Feet in stirrups, long boots blackened with shoeshine.
The evidence on the cards of a battle to begin.
Russia and Turkey across the Black Sea of early advance
                                        the horse's trot
Balaclava wisps of smoky huffs of smouldering hay.
The time to canter we, the British pull at our mares and geldings
We have dire need to break our horses in the way of warriors like
                                        us before them.
The thought of battle, the former the Russians and the latter of us
The British go forward into battle and gallop through.
Frenzied with thirst for revenge and a lick of blood.
With our dispatched money we buy more and more pistols.
Our trusty Winchesters spit lead up their faces.
To the bushes, to the bushes. Watch the Russians.
The number 401,272 acknowledged deceased.
Some without faces, some without limbs.
Rounding up the bodies, burying the dead.
Nightfall, my eyes twitch. Is there no victory charge?

Hardeep Singh Leader

HERO

What is a hero if not an ordinary man,
Who in extraordinary circumstances,
Does all that he can,
Who happens to be, by God's good grace,
There at the time in just the right place.

Carol Kendall

THE ULTIMATE WAR

Good versus evil
As old as the beginning of time;
Eve versus the snake,
God versus Lucifer,
The world versus man.

Where there is evil
There will be good to keep the balance;
Snow White versus the Evil Queen,
Ripley versus aliens,
Buffy versus vampires.

Sometimes evil may seem to win the battle
But good will always win the war.

Lindsey Brown

A FATEFUL DAY

It was a lovely summer day, the sun was shining bright,
But many folk who were working hard would not go home that night,
They were in a building targeted by some persons who were evil,
A plot organised that could only be thought of by the devil,
Terrorists boarded planes and captured crews and passengers there,
They told the crew their plans and all were filled with fear,
How ever did those people feel on that dreadful ride,
Knowing the plan was to fly the planes into the building's side?
Havoc was done, many people were killed on that fateful day,
Now how can any human being take the dreadful pain away.
Only God can give any sort of relief from that dreadful deed,
Which makes every sane human being's heart openly bleed,
Please Lord give these people relief from their dreadful pain,
And let them have the faith and trust in Christian love again.

Stan Gilbert

LORD, MY THOUGHTS FOR TODAY

Lord, I have had the most sad and lonely day,
The whole wide world seems to be in disarray.
The catastrophic disaster that happened in New York,
Brought the world to a standstill, everyone distraught.

Stunned by the vindictiveness of the onslaught
What satisfaction could it possibly have brought?
Killing ordinary people with families at home,
Rescuers working for hours, hearing the wounded groan.

With buildings so high, they had not a hope,
Fire bursting forth, trapped, how could they cope?
Some phoned home, before they were burnt to death,
Telling their loved ones, they loved them with their last breath.

Horrific, no other words could ever describe
How it must feel to be burnt alive.
Only God's people who lived in the last war,
We must not forget, what has happened before.

Hitler and his misdeeds came to an adverse end,
Let us hope these perpetrators get theirs, amen.
God said in his words, 'Vengeance is mine'
We must leave things to God, all will be fine.

Retaliation is not the way to go,
God forgave our sin, his grace we must show.
Is it the final battle between evil and good? (Armageddon)
We must turn to the Lord, we know that we should.

Sylvia M Harbert

SPACE HEROES

once you were shining
glowing like fireballs
you were swelling and soaring
you were dancing
dizzy with it all
sick with wonder
and delight

never holding back
taking it all in
like finding out
for you had to find out
you just had to
whatever it was

worlds upon worlds
subtleties of sensation
and feeling
aching to get to it
aching and yearning
for so long
but sometimes you couldn't hold it
and it slipped away from you

what strange
agonising journeys
you had
in these wonderful
dangerous worlds
the shining ones
beyond the stars

Julian Ronay

THE HIGHWAYMAN

In seventeen hundred and six one believes
In Hampstead a man was born
His youth he joined a band of thieves
Stealing cattle deer and fawn
He had a friend his name Tom King
They rode the roads together
Attacking robbing took everything
In all kinds of weather
They stopped the stage at a frightening pace
Sending chills to make one shiver
With a scarf tied tightly round their face
They shouted 'Stand and deliver'
Tom no more would shout and sing
For near the town of Dunstable
Dick accidentally killed Tom King
Whilst aiming for the constable
The London Yorkshire famous ride
On steed best known 'Black Bess'
He rode along the countryside
In searching for his quest
The outlaw's fate now caught in York
Found guilty of a theft
Then taken to a local court
He hung and there was left
This man whose exploits had begun
Now legend grew to fame
For he was 'The Highwayman'
Dick Turpin was his name.

Catherine Armstrong

THE INTRUDER

It comes upon a winter's night
This bandit of the air
Rushing round the skirting boards
And dashing up the stair.

It roves around in door jambs
In wild precarious fight
To get into the bedrooms
And rattle on all night.

It squeezes through the keyholes
And scampers from the door
Skips and trips around our feet
Then scurries o'er the floor.

It will sweep around for hours
Not resting for a minute
As it makes a home a chilly place
And everybody in it.

It whistles upon the chimney pots
And causes soot to fall
Then everybody quickly
Steps out into the hall?

Is there nowhere we can shelter
No place we can hide
No way we can keep
This fiend firmly outside?

David Sheasby

VILLAINS ON WHEELS

Up and down the road they go,
Not caring if there's rain or snow,
Making lots and lots of noise,
Gangs and gangs of girls and boys.

They scream and shout for all their worth,
There's nothing else like this on Earth,
You dare not stand outside and talk,
For fear they'll have you on the floor.

You need to be quick to avoid being hit,
And the lucky ones are the ones that are fit,
If you are disabled, you don't stand a chance,
And you won't even get a backward glance.

They're on you before you know where you are,
And they won't give a jot for freshly laid tar,
You tell them off and you get abuse,
Scooters should be rendered out of use,
I get them banging and ringing my bell,
And then they're gone like bats out of hell.

B Smith

CHARISMATIC HERO

He was nothing to look at
Though well groomed and smart
His ears were too big
His eyes wide apart

His hair was quite grey
Though distinguished and slick
His smile was enchanting
His movements quite quick

He'd that confident bearing
From time spent at sea
With the salt spray around
And the wind blowing free

He was full of good humour
So courteous and kind
But his temper was fierce
When injustice he'd find

The meeting at first
Was sharp and dramatic
And thirty years on
He was still charismatic!

Enid Gill

SUPERMAN

I am Superman,
Saving mankind from fiendish plan,
Hoping that no kryptonite,
Will sap my might,
For the forces of good I fight,
Faster than a speeding train,
X-ray vision embedded in my brain,
My girlfriend is Lois Lane,
I work for the Daily Planet,
As mild-mannered Clark Kent,
But when I see trouble that is meant,
I turn to a man of granite,
I saved the Earth,
From a speeding comet,
I'm so good,
You could vomit,
I save people from burnt-out cars,
And put a stop to nuclear wars,
And my day isn't complete,
If I don't help an old lady across the street,
So if you are stuck in trouble,
I will be there at the double,
Superman! Your one true friend
Who can save you from a sticky end.

Alan Pow

WISHFUL THINKING

Through all the times of trouble,
send the hero in.
Someone like Clint Eastwood,
handsome, tall and thin.
He moves just like a cat,
stalking out his prey,
and when it's time to act,
he blows the scum away.
And when he's done the job,
he rides into the sun.
I wish I was Clint Eastwood -
think I'll get 'the operation' done.

Ken Price

OMENS

Afghanistan
gentler than the wilderness
in Bin Laden
tilting his head
side to side
listening
listening and translating
the whistling wind
into voices
whispering depleted rhetoric
spent fuel from political combustion.
Weapons grade insanity.

People
The World Trade Center
alive only in memory.

He turns from the television
and slinks away
belly close to the ground
tail tucked under
body bent under the weight
of Omens.

The impending talons of a screaming eagle.
The throaty rumbling of a bulldog
drooling a destiny of teeth.

The Star Spangled people
are not alone.

Hamish Lee

C'MON GUYS, LET'S ROLL!

Who would ever have thought it possible
That mobile phones would change the course of history
For everyone to have one on their person today is cool
And there were many there among the passengers at Boston
On September 11, 2001 on the doomed United Airlines Flight 83

The terrorists who took over after take-off were so proud
of their fellow conspirators' successful massacre of thousands
earlier in the New York Trade Center
And so confident that they were on their way to another great
triumph with a similar destruction in Washington of The White House
That they allowed the use of the mobile phones by their hostages
in the cabin high up in the sky glad that through them news of their
infamous New York murders into the plane could enter
But unlike on the other terrorist flights that day
this was longer and gave
time for America's true fighting spirit among the hostages to arouse

Among the many heroes to come on that plane that dreadful day
we know the names of only three - Thomas Burnett, Jeremy Glick
and Todd Beamer
And they all knew they were destined soon to die
But they decided as men and brave Americans that they were not
going to give in to the murderers without a murmur or a stir
This was War and they would fight and not to give in lamely
to these thugs in the sky

With what must surely be a heroism quite unique in history they
quietly but quickly hatched their secret battle plan of campaign
Determined to do all they could to save the White House as the
symbol of all the Freedoms they and the whole Free World hold so dear
They would all together storm and overcome their captors and then
immediately take control and ditch the plane
This was War and they would now go to their certain death content
that they had died in fighting for their country and without fear

They had not a second to lose for any time now the terrorists' target
could come into sight
And it was Todd Beamer who got the job of Leader to give the signal
when to go
He wasted no time. 'C'mon guys,' he crisply said. 'Let's roll!'
And roll they did together into the fight
And we shall never know how hard it was for them to overcome
this murderous and blood thirsty terrorist foe

But win they did and a glorious victory high in mid air was theirs.
By overcoming the pilot and taking the controls they had caused
the plane immediately to fall
Not on its planned target to destroy The White House similarly
to the Trade Center towers
But at 9.58am as checked far away by the listener on Todd Beamer's
still operating mobile phone call,
This ill-fated United Airlines flight 83 crashed not to wreck more
havoc in Washington DC but upon an empty Pennsylvania field
and which henceforth must surely become a Memorial
Shrine for these heroes with monuments to them and blessed
with sacred flowers.

Frank Hansford-Miller

ADVENTURE KIDS

We will sit and watch the cinema screen.
Luke Skywalker and Darth Vader,
    you've every scene.
Shiny costume, tights and neat
No fighting to watch, it's such a treat.
Your favourite star sweetheart
    which you would slumber and meet.
All that adventure for us to see
    and isn't on TV.
Smiles oh, the scream, eating soft
    whip ice cream.
Babies sorted out, all the secret out again.
Wishing you could pay to see all
    watch it, it's the same.
Giving half a crown.
Shut and settled down.

Jay

POST

My excess baggage just won't go
    posted it many times
It just gets 'returned to sender'
    like poor repeating rhymes.

Couldn't it just be ejected?
    God's hold-all hold it all?
Yet thorn in the flesh piece was peace
    Grace reminder for Paul?

Robert D Shooter

TERRORISM

The madness of the few,
Cause havoc in the land,
Death and destruction caused by one hand,
The silent killer made his move -
With people all around,
The evil came from nowhere -
With just one thing in mind,
War at all cost never count the pain
Terrorists at work who had no shame,
Out of the sunshine, attack used two hijacked
                                    passenger planes,
The twin towers dropped to earth
With mayhem all around,
Shock and disbelief at what everyone had seen,
Why had this happened?
New York will never be the same,
Sadly this was not the end of this fateful day,
Two more hijacked planes were joining in the fray,
One crashed in Pennsylvania outside St David's Camp,
And one hit the Pentagon adding more victims
                                    to the count,
The evil came from nowhere,
With just one thing in mind,
Death and destruction of the cruellest kind,
Terrorists at work who had no shame
Brought the world to war again.

V Harding

BOW AND ARROW

As we rode through,
Sherwood Forest,
I wondered, how,
Robin Hood,
Could live in,
Such a big,
Wood.

I saw Errol Flynn,
When I was
Only a little
Muffin, I
Wrote to him,
A photo came,
With his smile,
On film.

We had a
Lovely day
In Nottingham.

B Brown

THE MOST UNHOLY ACT

Bending over his companion who's body
is lying broken on the ground
no fire engine will he ride again
no ladder more will climb
the siren call no longer hear
'twas the one that took him to the ground
the chaplain of his troop gives him
his final rites.
The demon act that caused such grief
brings the masonry crashing down on them,
killing the Minister in Holy Orders dead too,
whilst administering The Last Rite to a college
a Brave Heroic Fireman doing his duty.
On a day that will never be forgotten.

Margaret Gleeson Spanos

10,000 HEROES

I know ten thousand heroes
they're the folk that risk their lives
the police, firemen and ambulancemen
who face crashes, flames and knives
no one ever asked their names
just trusts that they'll be there
when danger strikes or ills befall
emotions laid so bare.
So sing the song of heroes
the champions of our lives
each one deserving medals
no bonus is their prize.
They do their job then vanish
no thanks they ask for all they do
they risk their lives each day and night
for folks like me and you.
God bless you each and every one
and thank you from the heart
where would we be without you
if your work you did not start?
You are such special people
so brave and selfless too
here's to ten thousand heroes
yes, you and you and you.

Channon Cornwallis

THE STADIUM

The stadium is alive it has a heart and soul.
Many memories it holds, from the days of old.
Even when it's empty, you can hear the roar,
When old Jackie Milburn used to score.

Stories of goals, matches they have played,
They are discussed on the terraces on match game days,
The chants and songs keep the spirit alive,
Names of players echoing through the skies.

The stadium comes alive, fans sing and roar,
Shouting at players, willing them to score,
Their voices echo through the stands,
People are shouting, clapping their hands.

The fans' loyalty will never die,
They have a spirit inside that keeps them alive,
To them it's not just a game, but a way of life,
They've seen their team, come through trouble and strife.

But when the floodlights go out, and everyone has gone,
You can still hear the fans singing their song.
Chanting vigorously into the night,
Until they go down the crowd corridor and out of sight.

Andrew Brian Zipfell

JOHN WAYNE

Four hours I watched the silver screen
As heroes came, then faded
But not one there fired emotions
That in me were long since jaded

Then at last there came from way out west
A man who would rise to fame
And all other men would envy him
The one they called John Wayne

This giant of a man stood tall
Not just in size, but pride
Back ramrod straight, jacket taut
Across his shoulders wide

On screen he fought all evil
Defending what was right
To the weak and the down trodden
He was their guiding light

To him they turned, their champion
On him they could rely
He had no fear of any man
Yet was not afraid to cry

So from childhood to adulthood
True grit he did impart
And although he's long since passed away
He lives on in my heart.

Don Woods

CARER

His gate is old:
Mossed timbers shrink and crack -
The frame warps in the sun.
Fittings no longer quite align:
Strangers here would struggle -
For them the latch would stick,
Bolt stubbornly jam.
He has the knack
And knows the ways of bolt and latch:
How the pull and twist must synchronise
To let the gate swing free.

It is the same with his lost wife:
Helping to ease a tragic life
That can no more align.

. . . And synchronising mood and time
He helps her day unwind.

P B Osada

LOWRY'S LANCASHIRE

Matchstick Man, aroused from sleep,
Painting previous fight in street,
Boots and tempers black as night,
Lodging house a flaky white.

Matchstick Man, stands, unseen,
Pencil sketching playtime scene.
Dark-eyed children, chasing round,
Offspring of industrial town.

Matchstick Man, collecting rent,
Lunchtime sketches on park bench.
Arden's Farm, then Acme Mill,
Hunger passes, paper fills.

Matchstick Man, alone with dreams,
Paints from memory seaside scene.
Grey green seas whipped by a gale,
Flake white sun, vermilion sail.

Betty Lightfoot

Knight In Shining Armour

I want just one special friend
To love and understand.
Not just an acquaintance,
Someone to hold my hand.
A man who shares emotion,
As well as intellect,
Someone to look up to
And to treat me with respect.
A man who could be weak enough
To be a baby in my arms;
He also should be strong enough
To soothe me with his charms.
A knight in shining armour
On a charger dapple grey,
I guess I'll just keep dreaming
'Til I meet him one fine day!

Sandra Lester

THE LOCAL BURGLAR

Woken rudely by a shrill but soft wolf whistle
The householder stirred briskly in a hustle
Soft but firm thuds hammered on his arch
The fowls protesting as if on the march.

Climbing up the roof
He espied a cloven hoof
'Could this be the god Pan
Or a donkey thinking it just can?'

Slowly but certainly he stealthily clawed
Inch by inch he gallantly pawed.
At last he grabbed a hairy hand
Belonging to the beaming face of a local firebrand.

Panting with perspiring pools of sweat
Both eyes narrowed bleakly at the sudden threat
At last the homestead owner enraged
Managed to find his voice assuaged.
'Do I presume you have lost your way
Or do I just ensure that you pay?

The firebrand growled and let out a hiss
'Aw, let me go I just collected an egg
Or should I grovel and start to beg?'

Lenin Chigbundu

King Coal Is Dead

I was old before I grew up.
We all were. Old people living
In an old valley, near an old town.
Forgotten. Sad-eyed children frolicking
Over once vibrant entities we called pits.
Buried bones and buried souls where
Once men toiled, and many despoiled.
Again.
Only a ghostly echo of migrated spectres.
Nothing is precious here anymore.
Not even the cricket pitch.

It is midwinter, bleak and barren.
I am no hero, just an abhorrent phantom
Returning to haunt my ancestors,
And mourn the loss of a dear friend,
Who was once emperor of this now desolate domain.
Tall, proud and strong.
A colossus of the cricket pitch,
The colliery and the snug.
Always willing to reminisce
Over a pint, and a pipeful of twist.
So now he is gone, to join his valiant comrades,
And once his brother in arms.
Even the graveyard echoes wistfully
With his nobility, humility and courage.
A defiant valediction they cannot deny.

N A Wilford

HEROES OF BOYHOOD

I remember a book, my parents they bought,
When I was nine or ten,
It was a book about knights and King Arthur,
With stories so wondrous then.

That's what I believed in those innocent days,
As I read of those knights of old,
Yes read them and read them, all over again,
Just to 'see' all the stories unfold.

Don't know if I had just one hero!
King Arthur with special sword!
Remember the magic Excaliber,
Which gave enemies just reward!

But was it Sir Galahad or Lancelot,
Who did such chivalrous deeds,
That were my real heroes of boyhood,
Always riding on milky white steeds.

They rode out from great fortress castles,
Always having high walls and wide moat,
Where coloured pennants fluttered on towers,
And jousts fought, wearing Helm and Surcoat.

In those days as a child, many stories I read,
Of fights, for right over wrong.
Where the heroes always beat villains,
And the days full of magic and song.

The ways of King Arthur, and Round Table knights,
And the principles they upheld,
Perhaps were just legend, or were they?
For life long, in my thoughts they have dwelled.

Jay Smith

TWIN TOWERS

Twin towers of faith in commerce and prosperity
rear skywards, mankind's monuments to posterity.
Or so it seemed until the villains of the piece
broke that faith and that of every decent creed.
So many died before they sought release,
snuffed out by men with minds sick and diseased.

Wild images of planes in headlong flight,
erupting flames cruel burn from day to night
as ash like a volcano in eruption
spewed out its message of corruption,
this awful grey-black choking cloaking shroud.

Hijacked: two planes; a venerable religion.
Feeding hate, avoidance and suspicion
where mere appearance was itself a wrong,
the innocent deemed guilty without trial.
Now the weakened villains must face the strong,
transfixed on their crooked cross of self-denial

As from killer bees honeyed sweetness came,
so blackguards, in their everlasting shame,
conjured heroes from the ground that day.
But sadly all their help was to the dead
who rested in shocked debris, not cold clay
and loved ones lay uneasy in the bed.

From these grim ashes twin towers will rise again
to help to free the memory of its pain.
Towers of co-operation and redress
so such events cannot happen again.
Avenging hands will leave their palm impress
to cover and then wipe away the stain.

Norman Meadows

PERCEIVED SOCIAL EVIL

Perceived social evil!
Who are the perceivers
In this perceived social evil?
The walking blinded!
Blinded in a blinded society!
The facts kept at arms length!
The brave who dare to touch!
Dumbed minds who listen too much!

Vincent Rees

Autumn In Manhattan

We all thought the new century would bring
a brave new start.
A bright new world to every heart.
Yet not it seems to evil men
intent on causing world mayhem.
Evil people whose lives it seems
never nurture human dreams.
But I would say to this evil creed
that I have dreams.
Oh yes indeed.
Hopes that all people far and near
can lead their lives free from fear.
These evil sects can never hide.
May their hiding places be denied
till justice is given to all who died.
To families who have mourned and cried.

Maureen Reynolds

MY HERO

When no one seemed to care,
He was there.
Through all the aggression and pain,
And times I thought I'd go insane,
I felt as if I was not alone.
It looked as if I was on my own,
But deep down inside I think I knew,
He'd be the only One to carry me through.
My marriage lasted just over twenty-six years,
Strange how that fact didn't calm my fears.
Where had the man I married gone?
Because of my children I soldiered on,
Longing for that moment of release,
To feel contentment and to know peace.
I didn't have the courage to fight my way out,
I just succumbed to whatever came about.
Until that day when I knew I couldn't take anymore,
That's when He upheld me as I sobbed through to my core.
He showed love and how much my life was worth,
How He'd been with me since my birth.
I didn't really want a divorce,
I wanted my husband to change of course.
I had to accept that I was partly to blame,
And face the fact things could not be the same,
As they'd been the happy early days of our marriage.
So when he divorced me I summoned the courage,
By knowing that with His help I could get through.
Now He's in my thoughts in nearly everything I do.
He's my real life hero Who's with me wherever I go,
His name is God as I think you already know.

Rosina L Gutcher

LUNY LANDER

Waltzing wheels and galaxies
The music of the spheres,
Sway upon a night of seas
Fathoming the years and
Decked about with Earth light
Come the dancing goon,
Embracing distant star shapes
In the mountains of the moon.

Roger Mosedale

ONE HERO . . . TOO LATE!

As I wend
My way through life
Too many villains
Have caused me strife

The villains are so clever
And very cunning too
They came in many guises
I just didn't have a clue

Be careful of the
So called 'friend'
Because they could
Destroy you in the end

Listen to your heart
And listen to your head
The voice that is inside
'Careful where you tread!'

Not many heroes
Have come my way
Or maybe I didn't listen
To what they had to say

Now as I sit and reflect
I am filled with regret

That all too late
I realise

My mum was a hero in disguise!

Tricia Layton

WARTIME HERO

He was an hero, many years ago
People flocked round him, and loved him so
He came home on special leave, one Friday night
To tell people of the news, but not to take fright

He pleaded for them, to go in the air raid shelter
Because bombs were going to be dropped in the area
Without an argument, they done what they were told
They trusted this man, who knew him, of old

They went into the shelters, but, fear came that morn
Bombs hit their homes, and exploded till dawn
Houses were in ruins, and bombed to the ground
Their lives were spared, but they looked sadly around

Douglas Joe was in the airforce, a fine man was he
Who had knowledge of the bombs, and knew what was to be
Many people were rescued of their calamity that day
When bombs came fiercely down, on houses of four to their dismay

Joe has long ago, passed away, and peacefully sleeps
Way past the clouds, in Heaven under God's keep
He will always be a hero, in my heart, and mind
For, Joe was my dad, who was thoughtful, and kind.

Jean P Edwards McGovern

THE MASKED OUTLAW

He robbed the bank at gunpoint,
and galloped out of town.
The sheriff and his posse,
tried to track him down.

No one saw his face,
the outlaw wore a mask.
They didn't know his name,
to complicate the task.

His tracks were leading north,
along a mountain trail.
He knew if he was caught,
he'd end up in jail.

He headed for some cover,
where he had hid before.
His only hope of freedom,
was to outsmart the law.

He was kinda worried;
there was twelve of them.
So he hid the money,
in-case, they caught him.

He found a place to hide,
and as they raced on past.
He watched them disappear,
then pulled down the mask.

Martin Snowdon

The Dangerous World

Those shining towers rose above the Manhattan sky,
A giant tuning fork for the money we buy,
Standing so proud, in a peaceful world,
No one knew what would be unfurled.

What treacherous villainy have we spawned?
What vile hatred on democracy dawned,
Genocide, theft, destruction and fear,
Wrought by fanatics, which cost so dear.

America stopped, aghast and shaken,
Their proud liberty should never be taken,
How could this be, are we at war?
Our world's collapsing, why what for?

The shock and terror of this vile act,
Thousands murdered, the Pentagon cracked.
Mayhem and fire in New York streets,
Sorrow and sadness, courageous feats.

Pandemonium raining rubble,
Manhattan Island has big trouble,
A twisted pile of concrete and steel,
New York's on fire, this cannot be real.

Terrible images around the globe,
Terrorists invaded our abodes,
Stole our planes, killing our friends,
A vicious enemy can't make amends.

The earth is saddened by this deed,
People of every colour and creed.
We stand together against shadowy foes,
The net will close on those sick 'heroes'.

In the name of any God this is wrong,
No religion here, on the Devil's prong.
How can you sleep purveyors of death?
Where can you run to? East or west?

Someone is guilty, someone must pay,
This dirty dog has had his day.
He's bitten off more than he can chew.
Him, and his lethal flying crew.

People of this world unite,
Somehow we're going to win this fight
Never again must terrorism win,
It's evil, sadistic and a massive sin.

We're miles away from this awful mess
Our hearts are with you, may God bless,
He'll mend your sorrow, heal your scars,
Unite your families, make them stars.

Those shiny towers must rise again,
A monument to stand through wind and rain.
A proud democracy, straight and true,
A peaceful world for me and you.

Brian Hurll

ANGELS

The student nurse fastens here starched white apron,
And fixes her cap;
Walks onto her ward, there are breakfasts to be served,
Sister says hurry up; Matron will be along shortly,
Consultant with retinue of student doctors,
Patrols his patients,
As years pass, changing buckles with gained experience;
Passing exams,
Our society progresses with changes of uniform,
Through the decades,
Bright murals enrich the wards, gone are the
Regimented regimes,
Monitors are watched with experienced eyes,
Primarily still nurturing the life force.

B Tallowin

A CAMPING HOLIDAY - TRUE LIFE

The weather, cold and miserable.
The tent was very cold.
My loved ones just gone for a stroll,
and I was all alone.
Looking out the window.
I saw a couple go on board,
a converted van that's all.
A fire broke out, I saw it start.
I shouted, 'Fire! Fire! Fire!'
People came from everywhere.
I couldn't find the door.
The people were still inside.
A brave young man,
in leathers pulled the couple out.
They were still alive, 'Thank God'.
A hero he became.
I took charge of all, that needed to be.
And the newsmen just arrived.
The people formed a bucket chain,
and put the fire right out.
They didn't think the danger.
They could of blown sky high.
People were so sensible and
all worked as a team.
The fire was out, the couple looked after
before the police and fire
and ambulance arrived.

Heather A Breadnam

COCK OR HEN?

A long time ago, when we were young and carefree,
my father played a game with us with grass:
We would be walking up Merry's Gill which is a local field.
He would pull the grass out from under the bush,
then he would ask, 'Cock or Hen?'
If the grass-seed was bushy, it was a 'hen'.
If it was smooth, it was a 'cock'.
My father was always there in everything we did
when we were growing up.
My dad and mum brought me back to life again
when I died for five minutes in a road crash.

Barry Welburn

WITHOUT

I now know that out of sight is out of mind,
As I sit here crouched with all my sorrow,
Crawling into corners and holes that I find.
Praying for the day I won't wake up tomorrow.

Maybe I just want to breathe, did you think of that?
People always reminding me of my place.
maybe I don't want to hide, being used as a mat.
Looking and staring as if I were a different race.

What you cannot see, cannot be real.
People walk by with their blind eyes turning.
What you cannot touch, you cannot feel.
As I sit and huddle, constantly yearning.

Nobody chooses to hear my calls or cry,
I just need a shoulder and that's the case.
No one wants to answer my questions why?
I just need someone to care, a friendly face.

All this seems too much to ask of you,
Sorry to waste your time, but that's all I have.

Jamie Barnes

IF I RULED THE WORLD

Well let me think
If I ruled the world
No boat would sink
Nor babies stink
Wouldn't that be great?

Then again, might I add,
A small calculation
I wouldn't allow being sad
Or for that matter getting mad
That means parents too!

Because might I say
There's always one,
Parent not so gay
It's not so bad in May
Cos they're all out on the town!

Everything would be perfect,
Everything would be right,
Everything would change,
But just overnight
Like magic!

Jodie Ramshaw (11)

IF I RULED THE WORLD

If I ruled the world,
I'd cover it in flowers,
Lilies, poppies, pansies, roses,
You name it, there'd be thousands!

I'd rule out all the killing,
Make the fighting stop,
I'd get rid of all the noisy cars,
And all the motor shops.

There'd be no such word as bullying,
The world would be a peaceful place,
It would be such a joy to live in,
Life is not just one big race.

The world is our life,
Our blood, our soul,
And I would do anything,
To keep it alive and well.

Rose Cresswell (11)

IF I RULED THE WORLD

If I ruled the world, there'd be new laws,
There'd be lots of changes to fix the flaws.
If I ruled the world, there'd be no more war,
There'd be no fighting, if only we saw.

If I ruled the world, there'd be better lives,
There'd be no guns, no bombs, nor knives.
If I ruled the world, there'd be better news,
There'd be better clothes, bags and shoes.

If I ruled the world there'd be quieter trains,
There'd be better roads, with bigger lanes.
If I ruled the world, there'd be better food,
There'd be more people in a better mood.

If I ruled the world, there'd be no more crooks,
There'd be no more dark alleys, crannies and nooks.
If I ruled the world, there'd be better TV,
There'd be better qualifications, to put on your CV.

If I ruled the world, there'd be a happy face,
There'd be people of every race.
If I ruled the world, I would be good,
I'd be kind, fair and generous, like every ruler should.

Elizabeth J Roach

IF I RULED THE WORLD

If I ruled the world there would be no fighting,
No war only peace and harmony,
Everything would be free, with no poverty,
Everyone would have what they always wanted.

If I ruled the world,
Black and white people would be treated the same,
There would be more police and less crimes,
If I ruled the world it would be a perfect place.

Sarah Jane Quinn (11)

WILDLIFE

The birds are chirping in the trees
The dolphins jumping in the seas.
The wind is blowing the pretty flowers
For all of those long twenty-four hours.

The cold rain and the hot sun
Make me want to have some fun.
So let's go outside and play
Let's have some excitement today.

The animals scram, when darkness appears,
They run to their den.
And when the sunshine comes to them
They wake up and do it all over again.

Michael Hart (10)

IF I RULED THE WORLD

If I ruled the world
I would be famous,
To sing on stage and TV,
To have crowds flocking around,
Just to see me.

If I ruled the world
I would stop all wars,
So our world could be safe,
And so our children won't have
To see the violence we have seen,
Everyone could live in peace and harmony.

If I ruled the world
Everyone would be treated equally,
Nobody would be treated higher or lower,
Nobody would be discriminated against
Because of their colour or religion,
And no child or adult would be beaten or killed!

If I ruled the world
I would be with the people I love and like,
Forever and ever.

If I ruled the world.

Amey Welch (12)

IF I RULED THE WORLD

If I ruled the world it would be a wonderful place,
Everyone would have a big smiley face,
I'd make all the people happy and glad,
No one will be lonely and sad.

If I ruled the weather I'd make it rain,
So all the poor countries could grow their grain,
And after the rain I'd make the sun shine,
So we would all be warm and fine.

If I ruled the food there would be plenty to spare,
So we would all be able to share,
No one would be hungry or thirsty at all,
Whether fat or thin, short or tall.

If I ruled the world there would be no pain,
If I ruled the world and I'll say it again,
Now I'm just one person but listen to me,
To change the world we all have to agree!

Daniel James Connor Sutherland (8)

MUM

I have a mother who is just a little baggy
Now she's getting on, some things are getting saggy
I have known her for thirty years or more
For every one of my years, she's added three or four
It's not that I've been bad, or difficult for her
I've kept the straight and narrow, only accidentally erred
But somehow on the way, I've hit the usual trouble
And Mum is always there - now her trouble load is double
With comforting arms when a favourite toy is broken
A sympathetic ear after boyfriend's harsh words spoken
With bravery to lend when exam results arrive
A patient, frightened passenger when learning to drive
Waving her good wishes on work's first nervous day
Sharing celebrations when I get my first month's pay
Now I've left the nest with a new home of my own
I know that she's still there for me in person or by phone
When I'm married and a mother in my own right
If I'm half as good as she is, I'll know I've done all right!

Tracy Enright

SIDE BY SIDE

They sang as they worked:
The young 'Canary Girls'.
Munitions factory women.
Deserters of the kitchen
Who worked at their benches,
Side by side.

For twelve long hours they'd struggle:
Their aching backs bent double.
Loyal and uncomplaining.
Their duties never shirking
As they worked at their benches,
Side by side.

'Shells made by a wife
May save a husband's life'.
This slogan they would prattle
As they helped to win the battle
By working at their benches,
Side by side.

Yet not without its cost,
For many a life was lost
Amongst munitions workers:
The handlers of explosives
Who worked at their benches,
Side by side.

They sang as they worked:
The young 'Canary Girls'.
As their skin changed its colour
To a dull shade of yellow
Through working at their benches,
Side by side!

Sandra Wolfe

WHAT PRICE VALOUR?

A whistle blast echoed the mist, one
cold November morn,
the youth held tight his frightened
tears, lest they might wake the dawn.

For 'tis then he runs the race of death,
with life the only prize, and prayer his
only protection, should God then heed
his cries.

From the mud he climbs, and begins to
run, through the mist, and rain, and shell,
he runs on wings of terror born, into
a living hell.

The barbs of steel embraced shim, when
came the bullet's kiss, and there his young
young life ended, as he gazed into death's abyss.

His tears, like many that cried that
day, were lost in the crimson mud. His
memories, dreams and promises, all
flowed with his precious blood.

'Neath clouds of rain they were found.
The dead, and those still praying for life.
Their cries 'tis said, are heard to this day,
for mother, for brother, for child, for wife.

Then silence fell on Flanders' fields, as
the guns all ceased to roar. But for the
youth, the flame had died, his laughter
heard no more.

Red poppies grow now on Flanders' fields, in memory of
those who died, and where one cold November morn, the
angel of death had cried.

Jim Cuthbert

THE DREAM

I had the strangest dream the other night,
I saw an angel shining bright,
An open book held in his hands,
In which he wrote in golden bands.

I studied him with great delight,
As curiously I watched him write,
And as he made a further note,
I asked him what it was he wrote.

He looked at me as there I lay,
And then it was I heard him say,
'I write of those who can afford
To say with pride, I love the Lord.'

I lay there in my earthly bed,
And thought awhile before I said,
'Put me down with your golden pen
As one who loves his fellow men.'

He wrote - and in a flash was gone,
But returned before the night was done,
I guess I must have passed the test,
Because my name led all the rest.

G K (Bill) Baker

HEROES AND VILLAINS

Heroes come in many forms.
Heroes weather many storms.
Some are carers every day
Suffering hardships come what may.

Often heroes want no praise.
Often heroes endure days
Of criticism and rebuff
When actions never are enough.

Heroes are found in every town.
They always help us when we are down.
Heroines, too, we must include.
In times of need they can exude

A calming presence to us all.

Villains on the other hand
Can be quite a different band.
Destruction often is their aim,
Themselves not taking any blame

For actions which they instigate,
Often planned in times of hate.
They'll make excuses for their means.
Perhaps this starts when in their teens?

They seem determined to destroy
The pleasures other folk enjoy
Regardless of the hurt or harm.
Their attitude causes alarm

To everyone except their group.

Catherine Craft

YOUR COUNTRY NEEDS YOU

What value do you rate a 'veteran'?
Is it by diamonds or gold?
When thrown in the cauldron of warfare
Facing terror and torment untold.

What then the key to survival,
This desire and the will to prevail,
When facing all odds stacked against one,
Intent on provoking travail?

My own recollections are hazy,
When wondering why I'm still alive.
Though conscious there are 'guardian angels'
That do ward off trouble and strife.

But what puzzles me so intensely,
Is what values are placed on the act,
Of giving one's life for just causes,
And then to come home to the fact,

That, for all of the services rendered,
As at the 'Cenotaph' down in Whitehall,
Heroes are taken for granted,
Two minutes, and that says it all.

Two minutes' silence . . . per annum!
Is that such a great deal to pay?
Honouring those very brave heroes,
That are no longer with us today.

> To all living souls in Great Britain
> A message to each as of now.
> *Two minutes silence is golden*
> If only to honour a vow.
> *'When you go home, think of us and say,*
> *For you tomorrow, we gave our today!'*

D Turberfield

MY SACRED FLAME

You made my heart sing
    like a young gazelle -
How great a mystery
    the hand of God -

You brought to me
    all heaven's sweetness
You took away -
    life's misery.

You walked alone in
    heaven's garden -
You bore our sin before
    our time -

You touched my heart
    and beckoned onwards -
I draw nearer still in
    Jesus' name.

I love you Lord
    and how my heart sings,
Forever I'll follow -
    my sacred flame!

Mary Skelton

BIG JOHN

Always the winner in our eyes
Not kissing girls till the end
His guns winning the prize
Bad guys their ways had to mend

His eyes just like slits as he
Fought with his gun
Living on his wits
Helping some poor mother's son

Cavalry he would command
Always the orders to give
With a commanding wave of his hand
Not letting the Indians live

His like has gone
Forever I fear
But his fame will live on
With us who held him dear

We scan the pages of television dates
Hoping that he will be there
Then baddies will go to their fates
For two hours or so we can share

Riding the range with our hero
Shooting bad men with him
Boredom at absolute zero
Eyes slightly tearful and dim

The man was a colossus to me
He looked just the part on his horse
A cowboy to all who could see
His name - John Wayne of course.

John Of Croxley

JASI

How the butter can melt in one's mouth,
And how Mother Nature can hold you in her arms,
So pure, bright budding child,
Open up and unfold,
Jasi, you are my future, I hold.

There's no treasure on Earth,
I can compare,
When in despair you are always there,
There is love, there is hope,
There is eternal light,
Jasi, you are my future bright!

A Bhambra

LIVE WIRE

(Dedicated to Louise Gold and Una Brandon-Jones,
two very sparky actresses)

All of a sudden
The place is alight
That's the missing spark
Nineteen ninety-eight's
Lost musicals lacked.

All was plain and then,
That spark made it bright.
The contrast is stark.
Live-wire Louise
Really makes her mark.

She's electrifying
As the song says, *if,*
you want to start a fire
you just have to *wire*
Our *Panama Hattie.*

With glorious voice,
That soars as a lark
Like *Burgundy rolled,*
Over the footlights
Her lyrics are sent.

Acting or Puppeteering
That spark of pure *Gold,*
Ms Brandon-Jones's
Bundle of talent,
Is a *real live* girl.

Emma Dorothy Shane

MACBETH

You killed a king to be a king;
Ambition screamed for you as king,
From lips of one who'd be a queen,
And helped you thus to kill a king.

> Three witches said you'd wear a crown,
> Temptation lured you to a crown;
> But first you had to kill a king,
> To snatch your strangely promised crown.

The ghosts you made to rule a realm,
Showed you ill-made to have a realm;
But conscience hovered in your crown,
And, widowed, lone, you held your realm.

> But woods may walk towards a king,
> As you discovered, as a king.
> For he who steals a royal crown
> Must learn to live, and die, a king.

And he who's born to kill his lord,
Must track his star to kill his lord;
Thus as you killed to gain the crown,
So did Macduff kill you, his lord . . .

Anne Rolfe-Brooker

THE KAMAKAZI DRIVER

The kamakazi driver we've all seen him around
He goes round every corner with two wheels off the ground.

At red lights he's a menace, his engine roaring wild
He could be almost any age, but acts like he's a child.

His mobile phone is at one ear, one hand upon the wheel.
The loudest music ever heard, he plays with greatest zeal.

When changing his direction, doesn't indicate which way
And if you misread his intent, then beware the price you'll pay.

He won't extend his courtesy to drivers of the road.
He'll abide by only his own rules and not the Highway Code.

If you think this sounds familiar, absurd, or just untrue
Then just make absolutely sure, that driver isn't you!

Christine Lannen

Unrewarded Heroes

What do heroes look like?
Are they short, fat, long or thin?
They come in various sizes,
All types - all colours of skin.

Their acts go unrewarded.
Some do not even know
How much they are respected.
They just arrive and go.

What would we do without them?
They help us out of mess
In times of serious trouble
They face up to the test.

They're brave, they're calm, they're thoughtful.
Their courage really shows.
Without these valiant heroes
Our lives would quickly go.

Doris E Pullen

SALUTE TO JANE AUSTEN

If I were cast away on an island
All by myself for a year and a day,
Nowhere to go and no one to talk with,
Here's what I'd do to enliven my stay -
Build a shelter not far from the shoreline,
Study the flora and fauna nearby,
Laze in the sunshine reading Jane Austen;
O, how the hours and the minutes would fly!

Twelve months of exile - more like an idyll;
Who could be lonely in such company?
Elinor, Anne, Elizabeth, Emma,
Catherine, Fanny, your faces I see,
And in your fortunes, your hopes and your fears,
I could be happy for many long years.

Sheila Burnett

THE 999 TEAM

They are the unsung heroes,
They are the ones who save lives,
They give help and comfort and support.
Support to the injured,
Support to the families,
Comfort to the dying.

They are the first on the scene,
The ones who do not ask for praise,
The ones who ask for nothing more than
To be there in a time of need.
Always strong, reliable and kind.

They are the 999 team,

Fire - Police - Ambulance.

Janet Cavill

HEROES AND VILLAINS

Robin Hood, Robin Hood and his merry men
Robin Hood, Robin Hood and his band of ten
To give to the poor they took from the rich
They hid in the trees and lay in the ditch
With feathers in caps and dressed all in green
They blended in with the woods difficult to be seen
For the Sheriff of Nottingham they lay in wait
He and his men could meet their fate
He was mean, didn't care for the meek
That is why Robin and men the Sheriff did seek
Little John, Friar Tuck to name but a few
They are together in the job that they do
Robin's been captured but freed by his men
With lots of followers three score and ten
They were faithful to Richard he was their King
Fought by his side peace for to bring
Not forgetting Maid Marian she was the King's ward
Given her hand in marriage that was his reward
After peace was restored Robin regained his land
And was knighted by Richard - well done to the band!

Brownie

THE BULLY

Persecuted from nine to three,
from bell to bell from lesson to lesson.
Darting from one class to another,
hiding from the school's self appointed big brother.
He'll steal your money; he'll poke fun and make you feel a disgrace.
He does not understand he scars for life the mind of the child
                                                    he oppressed.

David Bilsborrow

AMERICAN HEROES

Struggling to move its train
With four cylinder energy
Chuck Berry tunes his guitar
To the locomotive's 'woo woo' whistle
And clanging bell
The Wilson brothers
Roar past in a dented convertible
Full of beach beauties
Its radio tuned to a dewop station
Young Jews doodle superman
On cafe menus
Ferlingheti looks
For inspiration
From desert dunes and sinking suns
As Jack Kervrac
Waves from a westbound fright.

Paul Wilkins

HERO OF HEROES

Was Robin the goodie, the sheriff the baddie?
And Harold, now would he have won, only had he
Not had that arrow from William's men
Go in his eye? And what about when
Peter taught Wendy to fly to the Land Never Never:
Home of lost boys, heroes against terror
Of Captain Hook's plots; and was David's sight
Set on casting lots to go out and fight
Goliath the giant? And what about Joan
Of Arc, so defiant to go it alone?
Then burnt as a witch for her courage and faith;
And Judas, for silver-kissed and betrayed
The hero of heroes; the lord of all lords . . .
Jesus, the Saviour! Crucified for
Loving and teaching; when He comes again
The age of the villain will come to an end.

Marion Skelton

ONCE UPON A TIME, HERD IN THE WILDERNESS

My major strength, said the detached voice
Is that I can, on occasion, become utterly tedious
And naturally you might think that could be a weakness
In a man among men
Yet consider that the voice which seems to have echoed
About mountain caves for aeons before becoming tediously audible
Through a freak horizontal fissure.
That voice has decades of thought built in.
Mainly about socialism and the rights of the common man.
And why bus drivers so frequently pleasant, drive so fiercely
Whilst we discuss Shaw and the education of the workers at the back.
Politics is the art of instant plausibility now, and anyone
Seen to pause for thought on a screen loses vote papers by the sheaf.
Whilst I read on metaphysics and dialectical materialism
With dusty demons like Lucifer
Or consider chess problems, holding a lit cigarette by the ear
They are all racing around losing their mentation
Or injuring their brains.
There's a lot of thought somewhere ahead,
Fashionable again possibly.

Michael C Soper

THE HERMIT

I'll stay locked away from all mankind,
And say that I've left the world behind.
But I won't lie down with my head on a block,
I'll be by myself to fully take stock.
Or until such a time as I have the strength,
To face the wicked world so tense.
In my hut of dark despair,
With courage I have mustered there.
I'll face the evil that abides today,
In our world, and won't go away.
I'll do my best to be cheerful and bright,
Make others happy by sharing their plight.

Val Bermingham

THE WORLD TRADE BUILDING

An ordinary day, light crept under the curtain
and diffused the room
the alarm clock set its strident call.
Time for work, time for school.

The usual cornflakes, one eye on the clock,
on with fresh trousers or floral frock,
down the path, take the train or bus
all routine smooth passage for all of us.

Take the lift to various floors
pick up the pen, commence one's chores
here the tune changes a discordant note.
Panic and fear tightens one's throat.

Noise, confusion, acrid smoke, choking dust.
How does one react, is there a plan
how to collect one's self in a moment's span.
Some rushed for the lifts while the building rocked

Some tried the doors, found them blocked.
Some tried the stairs, joining the throng.
The constant cry was, oh God
what's gone wrong

Those on high floors hadn't a chance in hell.
They hung out of windows, some hopelessly fell.
In the raging inferno girders buckled and slewed
death came in many guises both swift and crude

Do you suppose they knew their enemy
that came from the blue
did they cry out, oh God, what did I do.
Nothing my children, come home to my arms

I can but hold you and quell your alarm
my tears I shed for this act of war
shall become the world's biggest open sore
again in my name they bring terror and ruin
but this destruction was not of my doing

I sent my son, gentle, loving and kind
to teach man to be compassionate, fair in mind,
these are my children, to me they must answer.
I ask they look into their hearts, do they beat faster

For they shall be uncovered and stand naked before God
and learn there is nothing but blood where they trod
they left a legacy of hatred and fear
and for that, poor demented fools, they shall pay dear

For them no glory, no seat upon high.
Beware all terrorists, for justice is nigh.

Joan L Charles